Synopsis of Artificial Intelligence's History

Dissecting the Threads of Machine Intelligence

Koso Brown

Contents

Introduction

The Artificial Intelligence History

The goal of artificial intelligence, a field that has only been around for 60 years, is to mimic human cognitive capacities through various sciences, theories, and techniques (such as computer science, statistical analysis, probability, mathematical logic, and computational neurobiology). Started during the Second World War, its advancements are closely related to computing and have allowed computers to accomplish many intricate jobs previously limited to human performance.

Nonetheless, this automation is still very different from human intelligence in the strict sense, which is why some academics disagree with the term. The current state of achievement ("weak" or "moderate" AIs, incredibly efficient in their training field) is not comparable to the final level of their study (a "strong"

AI, i.e. the ability to contextualize quite varied specialized issues in a wholly autonomous fashion). For the "strong" AI that has only yet been seen in science fiction to be able to model the entire world, basic research advancements rather than only performance gains would be necessary.

Chapter 1: The Birth of Artificial Intelligence

The years 1940–1960 were characterized by a convergence of technological advancements—which were accelerated by the Second World War—and the quest to comprehend how to combine the operations of machines and living things. According to cybernetics pioneer Norbert Wiener, the goal was to integrate automation, electronics, and mathematical theory into "a whole theory of control and communication, both in animals and machines". Previously, as early as 1943, Warren McCulloch and Walter Pitts created the first mathematical and computer model of the biological neuron, known as the formal neuron.

Though they did not coin the term artificial intelligence (AI), John Von Neumann and Alan Turing were the forerunners of the field's technology, having moved from computers to 19th-century decimal logic (which handled values between 0 and 9) and machines to binary logic (which relies on

Boolean algebra and handles more or less significant chains of 0 or 1). Thus, the two researchers codified the architecture of modern computers and showed that they were universal machines that could carry out instructions.

However, Turing's famous 1950 article "Computing Machinery and Intelligence" raised the question of whether a machine could be intelligent in the first place. Turing also described a "game of imitation" in which a human should be able to tell in a teletype dialogue whether he is speaking to a machine or a man. Even though this piece is controversial—many experts don't seem to agree that the "Turing test"

qualifies—it is frequently credited as the catalyst for the ongoing debate about the boundaries between humans and machines.

According to Carnegie-Mellon University's Marvin Minsky, "artificial intelligence" (AI) is "the construction of computer programs that engage in tasks that are currently more satisfactorily performed by human beings because they require high-level mental processes such as perceptual learning, memory organization, and critical reasoning." "AI" may be attributed to John McCarthy of the Michigan Institute of Technology.

The discipline is credited with founding at the Rockefeller Institute-funded Dartmouth College meeting in the summer of 1956. Anecdotally, it is important to highlight the remarkable success of the workshop that replaced the conference. McCarthy and Minsky were among the six individuals who had remained constant throughout this study, which mostly relied on innovations based on formal logic.

Even though the technology was still exciting and promising, its popularity declined in the early 1960s (see, for instance, the 1963 paper "What Computers Can Do: Analysis and Prediction of Judicial Decisions" by California Bar member Reed C. Lawlor). Using a computer language was challenging because of the computers' small memory. However, some foundations were already in place and are still in use today, such as problem-solving solution trees. The information processing language, or IPL, allowed programmers to develop the logic theorist machine (LTM) program in 1956 to illuminate mathematical theorems.

Economist and sociologist Herbert Simon predicted in 1957 that artificial intelligence (AI) would defeat a human in chess within the next ten years, but the AI then experienced its first winter. After thirty years, Simon's vision turned out to be accurate.

The Expert systems

The 1968 Stanley Kubrick film "2001 Space Odyssey" has a computer called HAL 9000, which is just one letter apart from IBM's logos. It encapsulates all the ethical concerns surrounding artificial intelligence (AI): will it be a threat to humanity or a sign of great sophistication? Naturally, the movie won't have a scientific impact, but it will help popularize the idea, much like science fiction writer Philip K. Dick, who will never stop wondering if machines can ever feel emotions.

The first microprocessors were introduced at the end of 1970, and this is when artificial intelligence (AI) took off and the era of expert systems began.

The route was first established in 1965 at MIT with the DENDRAL expert system, which focused on molecular chemistry, and in 1972 at Stanford University with the MYCIN system, which specialized in blood illness and prescription medicine diagnosis. An "inference engine," the foundation of these systems, was designed to be a logical reflection of human reasoning. Through data entry, the engine produced highly skilled responses.

Promises of great development were made, but by late 1980 or early 1990, the enthusiasm would collapse once more. It took a lot of work to program such information, and between 200 and 300 rules, there was a "black box" effect where the machine's reasoning was unclear. As a result, development and maintenance became very difficult and, more importantly, faster and in many other less complicated and less costly ways were available. It should be remembered that the word "artificial intelligence" was all but banned in the 1990s, and even more subdued terms like "advanced computing" made their way into academic discourse.

Herbert Simon's 1957 prediction was realized thirty years later when IBM's expert system Deep Blue defeated Garry Kasparov in a chess match in May 1997. However, this achievement did not encourage funding and further research into this type of artificial intelligence. All potential moves were assessed and given weight in the methodical brute force algorithm that drove Deep Blue's operations. Although Deep Blue's defeat of humanity is still highly symbolic in history, it only addressed a relatively small area—the chess game's rules—and is far from being able to simulate the complexity of the entire universe.

A fresh bloom built on vast amounts of data and enhanced processing capacity

The recent surge in the field around 2010 can be attributed to two things.

1. Then came the realization that computer graphics card processors could calculate learning algorithms more quickly due to their extremely high efficiency.

Before 2010, the complete sample could take weeks to process due to the very iterative nature of the process. These cards' processing power—more than a trillion transactions per second—has allowed for significant advancement at a relatively low cost—less than a thousand euros per card.

2. Access to enormous amounts of data first. In the past, sampling had to be done by hand to apply algorithms for image classification and cat recognition. A quick Google search can now turn up millions of results.

In 2011, Watson, IBM's IA, defeated two Jeopardy winners thanks to this improved technological equipment, which has also increased financing and made certain notable public triumphs possible. 2012 will see the ability of Google X, the company's search lab, to have an AI recognize cats in a video.

This final task has required the utilization of over 16,000 processors, but the potential is astounding: a machine can discern between objects. 2016 saw AlphaGO, Google's artificial intelligence for Go games, defeat Fan Hui, the European champion, and Lee Sedol, the world champion, before AlphaGo Zero, the AI herself. Let us clarify that the combinatorics of the game of Go is far more significant than that of chess (more significant than the number of particles in the cosmos) and that such achievements in raw strength are not achievable (as demonstrated by Deep Blue in 1997).

From where did this miracle originate? It is a total departure from the expert system paradigm. The method has changed to be inductive; instead of coding rules as in the case of expert systems, it is now necessary to allow computers to independently find them through correlation and classification based on enormous amounts of data.

Deep learning appears to be the most promising machine learning technology for various applications, such as picture or voice recognition. To bring neural networks up to date, Geoffrey Hinton (University of Toronto), Yoshua Bengio (University of Montreal), and Yann LeCun (University of New York) decided to launch a research program in 2003.

With the assistance of the Toronto laboratory in Hinton, experiments carried out concurrently at Microsoft, Google, and IBM demonstrated that this kind of learning was successful in cutting the error rates for speech recognition in half. The image recognition team led by Hinton produced comparable outcomes.

Chapter 2: Effects of artificial intelligence on human decision-making, complacency, and safety in the classroom

We must comprehend what "ethical" means in the context of artificial intelligence and education. Finding out about the primary problems and potential unintended repercussions of using AI in education, along with other important factors, is vital.

The cost of innovation, consent challenges, abuse of personal data, criminal and malicious use, loss of freedom and autonomy, and the loss of human decision-making are some of the general ethical issues and concerns associated with AI.

However, technology also improves consumer interactions (Rasheed et al., 2015), competitive advantage (Sayed and Muhammad, 2015), and corporate information security (Ahmad et al., 2021).

There is a fear among researchers that by 2030, the AI revolution will center on improving benefits and societal control, but it will also bring up ethical issues that no one can agree on.

A distinct difference in opinion of AI's beneficial effects on morality and life (Rainie et al., 2021).

The literature on AI ethics makes clear that, in addition to its many benefits, the development of AI also brings with it several ethical issues related to, among other things, moral ideals, behavior, trust, and privacy.

The application of AI in education presents several ethical issues. Numerous researchers are delving deeper into the field. Three tiers comprise our division of AI in education. The technology itself, its creator, producer, etc., comes first. The effects on the learner or student come in third, followed by the teacher.

The development of AI technology for education must come first; this cannot be the source of moral dilemmas or worries.

The enormous expectations for AI have generated 400+ policy texts on ethical AI, sparking attention and worry worldwide. Thorough conversations on moral matters provide a useful starting point, readying scientists, administrators, legislators, and instructors for fruitful debates that will produce precise guidelines for creating dependable, secure, and reputable systems that will be profitable.

But the real question is: Is it possible to create educational AI that will never raise moral questions?

Perhaps the maker or developer of AI technology in education stands to gain dishonestly from it. It's possible that their goals are not to support and improve education.

I ask myself these kinds of questions whenever someone discusses the application of AI in education. There is no assurance that the opposing viewpoint will hold, even if the development of AI technology is free from any ethical considerations from the manufacturer or developer.

Technological excellence will also determine the risk of ethical issues. While higher-quality technology will reduce risk, can all educational institutions afford to use this costlier, higher-quality technology? Second, using AI technology in the classroom can lead to a lot of problems.

It could be implementation, usage, security, etc. I have concerns about prejudice, price, trust, security, etc.

Thirdly, user-level concerns include those related to privacy, trust, safety, and health. Policies and a strong regulatory framework are needed to handle such issues. Unfortunately, to date, no framework, set of agreed-upon standards, policy, or set of rules has been formed to address the ethical concerns highlighted by AI in education.

It's clear that there are a lot of worries about AI technology, and the education industry is no different from other industries in that regard.

Most challenges and problems have an impact on education either directly or indirectly, even if they don't all directly affect learning and education. Therefore, it is challenging to determine if AI will have a net positive ethical impact on education or a net negative, slightly positive, or negative impact.

The discussion of the moral implications of AI technology will go on from instance to instance and situation to situation.

Three ethical concerns with AI in education:

1. making people lethargic
2. Human decision-making is lost

3. Privacy and security

1. Making people lethargic

Artificial Intelligence is a technology that has a big impact on industry and is changing practically every element of society and human life. AI's growing influence in businesses and society alarmed people like Stephen Hawking and Elon Musk.

Who believes that there is a chance AI could become uncontrollable for humans once it reaches a high level of development? The fact that research grew eight times faster than other industries is concerning. The majority of businesses and nations make investments to develop and acquire AI knowledge, expertise, and training.

However, the main issue with AI adoption is that it lessens human control and complicates AI's role in sustainable value creation.

The ability of the human brain to reason will naturally be limited when AI is used more and more.

As a result, humans' ability to reason is gradually diminished. As a result, humans lose their ability to reason and become more artificial. Furthermore, our constant contact with technology has forced us to think inhumanely like algorithms.

The reliance of people in practically every aspect of life on AI technology is another problem. It has unquestionably raised living standards and made life easier, but it has also had a terrible effect on humankind, making people sluggish and irritable.

The human brain will eventually get starved of contemplation and mental effort as it dives further into each task, such as organizing and planning. When physical or mental measures are required, a high level of reliance on AI may deteriorate professional abilities, cause stress, minimize our autonomous function, replace our choices with its decisions, and make us lazy in many areas of our lives. There is a claim that AI erodes human autonomy and responsibility, which hurts contentment and pleasure. The effects will extend beyond a particular demographic or region to include the education industry. When working on a task or assignment, teachers and students will employ AI software or their work may be completed automatically. Addiction to AI use can eventually result in laziness and troublesome circumstances down the road.

2. Human decision-making is lost

Making decisions involves a lot of technology. It enables people to effectively use knowledge and information to make decisions that are appropriate for their organizations and ideas. Humans are producing vast amounts of data, and businesses are adopting AI and leveraging it to make the data more productive while preventing human use.

When humans use AI to make judgments, they believe they save time and obtain benefits.

On the other hand, it is surpassing human biological processors by lowering cognitive capacities. It is a reality that there are numerous advantages to AI applications and technologies. However, there are still several grave drawbacks to AI technologies, one of which is the reduction of their influence over human decision-making. AI eventually diminishes and takes the place of humans in decision-making. Decision-making is becoming less dependent on human mental faculties including critical analysis, creative problem-solving, and intuitive analysis.

As a result, they will lose out because of the proverb "use it or lose it." The use of AI in strategic decision-making processes has expanded from 10% to 80% in just five years, demonstrating the technology's rapid adaption.

AI is being used by Walmart and Amazon to make decisions about their products and to streamline their hiring processes. Furthermore, it's becoming increasingly involved in senior management choices.

AI is used by businesses to efficiently evaluate data and make difficult decisions to gain a competitive edge. Humans still have the last word in all decision-making, even though AI is assisting in many different areas. It emphasizes how crucial human interaction is to the process and how important it is to make sure AI technology and people collaborate. It is anticipated that in the future, the human–machine collaboration strategy will combine into a hybrid paradigm.

Every day, more and more educational institutions are using AI to aid in decision-making. Universities are using AI for both administrative and scholarly purposes. AI's major responsibilities in the education sector include personalization, tutoring, quick responses, 24/7 access to learning, question answering, and task automation. Students can now receive assistance from AI for everything from program admission requirements to degree issuing.

AI gathers information, evaluates it, and then acts—that is, makes decisions—in each of the aforementioned functions. It is necessary to pose a few straightforward yet crucial queries: Does AI have moral consciences? The response is that AI is racist, and its selection may not be morally right.

Does AI affect people's ability to make decisions? is the second query. Through the use of an intelligent system, candidates can send their records straight to the designer, avoiding human review, and receive approval for admission tests. The technology will be trusted by the authorities, which is one reason; task automation may also contribute to leaders' laziness.

In a similar vein, the system's decision-making about the maintenance of student records and data analysis will be based on trust or the sloth that task automation creates among the authorities. Teachers and other staff members almost always lose their ability to reason when making administrative or academic choices. And the AI systems the institution has installed are becoming more and more dependent on them every day. In summary, artificial intelligence (AI) automates processes and reduces the need for human intervention in decision-making and job execution within educational institutions. AI renders teachers and other administrative workers useless since it does so much of their work for them. They are losing the ability to perform standard activities in an educational setting, which leads to a loss of reasoning and decision-making skills.

3. Privacy and security

According to Stephen Hawking, the development of artificial intelligence will be the biggest development in human history. Sadly, if we don't figure out how to reduce the risks, it might also be the last. One of the main worries about AI and learning is security. Trust-worthy artificial intelligence (AI) in education: Promises and problems. AI technology is being used in the majority of educational institutions' curricula, and this has drawn interest from researchers. Numerous academics concur that artificial intelligence (AI) has a major impact on e-learning and education (Nawaz et al. 2020; Ahmed and Nashat, 2020). The current COVID-19 pandemic provides concrete evidence for their argument.

However, security and privacy are the major worries and difficulties that artificial intelligence (AI) and machine learning have brought to the education sector.

There's no denying that artificial intelligence (AI) systems and applications are finding their way into education and classrooms. Every tool has a certain function, and both teachers and students use it in that manner. Using voices to access information, creates an immersive learning environment and raises security and privacy concerns. While addressing a privacy-related query, the main focus is on student safety when it comes to AI devices and their use. This might also apply to the teacher's situation.

Massive amounts of data are gathered and used by AI systems to create patterns and predictions, yet there is a potential for prejudice and discrimination. These days, a lot of individuals are worried about the moral implications of AI systems and think that security needs to be taken into account while developing and implementing AI systems. The Facebook-Cambridge Analytica controversy is among the most notable instances of how technologically obtained data can raise privacy issues. The National Science Foundation acknowledges that a great deal of work has been done, but much more effort is still required. Kurt Markley claims that schools, colleges, and universities are vulnerable because they have large databases of student records that include information about their social security numbers, health, and payment details, among other things. To make data secure and stop data breaches, educational institutions must constantly review and redesign their security procedures. When information technology is used effectively or in distant learning situations, the problem is considerably more severe.

It's also critical to remember that with remote learning, security issues grow with networks and endpoints. One issue is that particularly in the school sector where funds for extracurricular activities are scarce, safeguarding e-learning systems against cyberattacks is neither simple nor inexpensive.

The fact that educational institutions employ relatively few technical staff members—hiring them is another financial concern—is another factor contributing to this serious threat. The problem is that not all teachers are professionals who are qualified to utilize technology or who can handle common hazards, even if adopting intelligent technologies like AI and machine learning can reduce security threats to some extent.

It's also critical to remember that with remote learning, security issues grow with networks and endpoints. One issue is that particularly in the school sector where funds for extracurricular activities are scarce, safeguarding e-learning systems against cyberattacks is neither simple nor inexpensive.

Conceptual structure

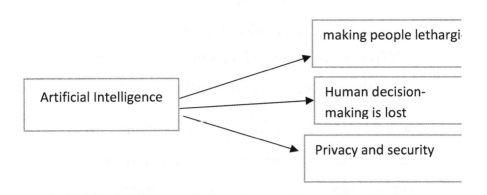

Artificial Intelligence and Human Prospects

Over the next ten years, experts predict that artificial intelligence will improve the lives of most people. However, many people are worried about how these developments will impact what it means to be human, productive, and capable of free choice.

Digital existence is both enhancing human potential and upending long-standing human customs. With ambient information and connection reaching over half of the world's population, code-driven systems present both unparalleled potential and hazards. Will people be better off than they are now when new algorithm-driven artificial intelligence (AI) spreads?

According to experts, networked artificial intelligence will increase human efficacy while simultaneously posing a threat to human agency, autonomy, and capabilities. They discussed the broad range of possibilities, including the possibility that computers could match or even surpass human intelligence and capabilities in a variety of domains, including speech recognition, language translation, advanced analytics and pattern recognition, smart decision-making, reasoning and learning, and visual acuity. They claimed that "smart" systems will save time, money, and lives and provide opportunities for people to enjoy a more personalized future in communities, cars, buildings and utilities, farms, and business processes.

Numerous speakers centered their upbeat remarks on healthcare and the plethora of potential uses of AI in patient diagnosis, treatment, and assisting elderly individuals in leading more fulfilling lives. They were also quite excited about the potential contribution of AI to large-scale public health initiatives based on the vast volumes of data on nutrition and personal genomics that may be collected in the upcoming years. Several of these academics also forecasted that AI would facilitate long-expected modifications to formal and informal education systems.

But whether they are pessimistic or not, the majority of specialists voiced worries about how these new instruments may affect fundamental aspects of human nature in the long run.

Chapter 3: Why has Artificial Intelligence come under fire?

Artificial intelligence can increase the efficiency of your company. That's triumphant. But regardless of the savings, raising your output could come at a cost. Putting AI ethics front and center will assist in guaranteeing that your company maintains its good status in terms of operations, regulations, and reputation.

Here are some Artificial Intelligence common issues:

1. **Keeping Competition and Ethics in Check:** Because there is never-ending competition to develop, new technologies pose a unique challenge to businesses of all sizes, including startups and IT giants. A company's ability to be the first to release a specific technology or application is often

what determines its success. Businesses frequently don't make the effort to make sure their AI systems are securely built or that they adhere to ethical design principles.

2. **Diminished Social ties:** While AI has the potential to improve customer service through chatbots and provide hyper-personalized experiences by tailoring search engine content to your preferences, there are worries that this could result in a loss of social connection, empathy for others, and overall well-being. You won't be able to cultivate an empathy-based mindset or take up socially conscious activities if all you see on social media are views that support your own.

3. **Intellectual Property Exploitation:** A recent case against ChatGPT, in which several well-known authors allege the platform used their copyrighted works illegally, has drawn attention to the problem of AI exploiting intellectual property.

Recently, OpenAI was sued by several authors—including well-known ones like Jodi Picoult and John Grisham—for allegedly violating their copyright by utilizing their writing as the basis for algorithm training. The lawsuit also asserts that authors' capacity to support themselves through their writing will be jeopardized by this kind of exploitation. Owners of intellectual property are worried about how AI will affect their livelihoods going forward due to this kind of exploitation.

4. **False information:** False beliefs and societal divisions can be exacerbated by misinformation, which can also be harmful to organizations and other people. Misinformation has come under increased attention in light of the recent political unrest since it has the power to sway public opinion and seriously harm a person's reputation. It can be difficult to track down the source of disinformation after it spreads widely on social media and is tough to

refute. Artificial intelligence (AI) tools have been used to disseminate false information, giving the impression that the material is reliable when it is not.

5. **Deepfakes:** The use of deepfakes raises moral questions. Voice and facial recognition are now vulnerable to deepfakes, which can be used to bypass security protocols. According to one study, deepfakes that are simple to create may fool a Microsoft API over 75% of the time. There are additional moral dilemmas with mimicry. Deepfakes can have a significant impact on public opinion when they are used to influence political elections. Concerns have also been raised about the possibility of using deepfakes to manipulate the stock market if a CEO was thought to be acting or making judgments that were seen as dubious. Because there is no control and the software is easily accessible, deepfake exploitation poses a serious security risk.

6. **Accountability:** Because AI is becoming more and more common in all industries, we use AI technologies regularly to make judgments. It can be challenging to assign blame for decisions that have unfavorable effects when they are made. Are businesses responsible for verifying the algorithms in a tool they purchase? Or do you turn to the person who created the AI tool? Maintaining people's and businesses' accountability can be challenging due to the deep rabbit hole that is the pursuit of accountability.

7. **Explainability:** It is insufficient to merely deploy AI tools and observe their effectiveness. In some AI applications, it can be very crucial to comprehend the decision-making process. Sometimes it's hard to understand the findings drawn by certain AI systems. This can have significant ramifications, particularly in fields like law enforcement and healthcare where real lives

are at risk and influencing variables must be taken into account.

8. **Security:** When it comes to AI, security is still of utmost importance (and any discipline of computer science). Inadequate security measures can have a broad effect. AI, for instance, is vulnerable to hostile attacks that could taint results. The Cybersecurity Infrastructure and Security Agency (CISA) cites cases where attacks cause autonomous vehicles to act inappropriately and when things are hidden in security camera footage. More security measures are being recommended by experts and governmental bodies to mitigate any potential harmful consequences.

9. **Bias:** AI bias raises yet another ethical question. Even while artificial intelligence (AI) is not intrinsically biased, systems are educated utilizing deep learning and input from human sources, which might result in

the spread of prejudices through technology. For example, if the data sets used to train the algorithm had prejudice against a particular group, an AI hiring tool may exclude certain demographics. If this results in discriminatory actions, legal ramifications may potentially follow.

10. **Privacy:** Large volumes of data are needed for AI model training, some of which contain PII. Concerns over who can access and use your data are raised by the lack of clarity surrounding its collection, processing, and storage. The use of AI in monitoring raises additional privacy issues. AI is used by law enforcement to track and monitor suspects' whereabouts. Despite their great value, many are concerned that these capabilities may be abused in public settings, violating people's right to privacy.

11. **Job Displacement:** One of the most common concerns raised in debates about AI is job displacement. There's concern that

automation will take the place of some or all job functions, driving up unemployment rates in particular sectors. As per the Business Technology Adoption and Skills Trends study by CompTIA, 81% of American workers have come across publications that discuss the potential replacement of workers with artificial intelligence. According to the same survey, three out of four employees are either extremely or moderately concerned about the effects of automated technology on the labor market.

What Actions are Undertaken to Control AI Technology?

The use of AI technology and its implications are yet somewhat unknown. As of right now, AI is not subject to any federal rules in the United States. However, there are already several rules in place that restrict the use of AI about discrimination, data protection, and privacy. Most businesses take care to at least abide by the CCPA and GDPR. Additionally, the White House unveiled a plan to introduce an AI

Bill of Rights that may offer more thorough guidelines.

The first comprehensive AI law in history, the AI Act, was recently passed by the European Union, also setting a precedent. China has created its own set of AI regulations, which are always changing. The regulation of AI is still in its infancy in the United States, and the majority of the laws that have been established are only implemented at the state level.

Is It Possible to Standardize AI Ethics Across Cultures and Regions?

It's possible that regional and cultural norms for AI ethics can be established. In 2021, the first global norm for AI ethics was created by UNESCO, an international body devoted to fostering world peace and sustainability. Companies should follow the guidelines in the Recommendation on the Ethics of Artificial Intelligence to guarantee that AI is used ethically. It is hoped that most nations will soon adopt these concepts, even though they have not yet been accepted by the global community.

Chapter 4: How the world is changing due to artificial intelligence

We suggest the following nine actions moving forward to optimize the benefits of AI:

1. Punish bad AI activity and encourage cybersecurity.

2. preserve systems for human supervision and management considers bias allegations carefully to ensure that historical injustice, unfairness, or discrimination in data or algorithms is not replicated by AI.

3. Govern general AI concepts as opposed to particular techniques,

4. Interact with local and state representatives to help them implement efficient policies,

5. Establish a federal advisory body on AI to draft policies.

6. Encourage the creation of innovative workforce development and digital education models so that workers have the

competencies required in the 21st-century economy.

7. Allocate additional public funds for unclassified AI research,

8. Promote increased researcher access to data while protecting users' privacy.

Characteristics of artificial intelligence

AI is usually understood to mean "machines that respond to stimulation consistent with traditional responses from humans, given the human capacity for contemplation, judgment, and intention," even though there is no universally accepted definition of the term. These software programs, according to academics Shubhendu and Vijay, "make decisions which normally require [a] human level of expertise" and assist humans in foreseeing challenges or resolving them as they arise. They therefore behave purposefully, wisely, and adaptably.

1. Deliberate Action

Algorithms with artificial intelligence are built to make judgments, frequently with the use of real-time data. They are not like passive machines, which can only react mechanically or in a predetermined way. They gather data from many sources, analyze it instantaneously, and take action based on the insights they gain by using sensors, digital data, or remote inputs. They can perform extremely sophisticated analyses and make extremely sophisticated decisions thanks to significant advancements in storage systems, processing rates, and analytical procedures.

2. Cognition

AI is typically used in conjunction with data analytics and machine learning.5. Using data, machine learning seeks out underlying trends. Software designers can use that information to investigate certain problems if it identifies something pertinent to a real-world scenario. All that is needed are data that are robust enough for algorithms to identify meaningful patterns. Digital information, satellite images, text, visual information, and unstructured data are some examples of data types.

3. Flexibility

AI decision-making systems possess the capacity to learn and adjust. For instance, semi-autonomous cars are equipped with sensors that alert drivers and other vehicles about impending traffic jams, potholes, road construction, and other potential obstructions. Without the need for human intervention, vehicles can benefit from the experience of other vehicles on the road, and the entirety of their acquired "experience" is instantly and completely transferable to other vehicles with comparable configurations. Incorporating knowledge of existing operations, its sophisticated algorithms, sensors, and cameras convey information in real time through dashboards and visual displays, enabling human drivers to comprehend traffic patterns and other vehicle circumstances. Furthermore, sophisticated algorithms are capable of operating a car or truck entirely and making all navigational decisions in fully autonomous vehicles.

Artificial intelligence applications across a range of industries

Artificial Intelligence (AI) is not a vision of the future; rather, it is a reality that is being incorporated into and used across numerous industries. This covers industries including banking, healthcare, criminal justice, national security, transportation, and smart cities. There are several instances when AI is already changing the world and significantly enhancing human capabilities.

Artificial Intelligence (AI) is not a vision of the future; rather, it is a reality that is being incorporated into and used across numerous industries. This covers industries including banking, healthcare, criminal justice, national security, transportation, and smart cities. There are several instances when AI is already changing the world and significantly enhancing human capabilities.

The enormous potential that artificial intelligence (AI) offers for economic growth is one of the factors contributing to its increasing prominence. "Artificial intelligence technologies could increase global GDP by $15.7 trillion, a full 14%, by 2030," according to a PriceWaterhouseCoopers report.

$1.2 trillion for Africa and Oceania, $1.8 trillion for North America, $3.7 trillion for China, $0.9 trillion for the rest of Asia outside of China, $0.7 trillion for Southern Europe, and $0.5 trillion for Latin America are among the advances that are included in this figure. China is advancing quickly because it has declared a national objective to invest $150 billion in AI by 2030 and take the lead globally.

Chapter 5: Transportation

One sector where AI and machine learning are leading to significant advancements is transportation. According to research conducted by Brookings Institution researchers Cameron Kerry and Jack Karsten, between August 2014 and June 2017, approximately $80 billion was invested in autonomous car technology. Applications for autonomous driving as well as the fundamental technology essential to that industry are included in such investments.

Cars, trucks, buses, and drone delivery systems are examples of autonomous vehicles that make use of cutting-edge technology. These features include automated braking and guidance, lane-changing capabilities, the use of cameras and other sensors to prevent collisions, real-time information analysis powered by artificial intelligence, and the ability to adapt to changing conditions using intricate maps powerful computers, and deep learning systems.

The keys to navigation and collision avoidance are

artificial intelligence (AI) and light detection and ranging systems (LIDARs). Radar and light instruments are combined in LIDAR systems. They are installed atop vehicles that use a 360-degree imaging system consisting of laser beams and radar to gauge the distance and speed of objects in the surrounding area. These instruments, along with sensors on the front, sides, and rear of the car, offer information that enables fast-moving cars and trucks to stay in their lane, avoid other cars, and apply brakes and steering instantaneously to prevent accidents.

To avoid the automobile in the adjacent lane, these cameras and sensors gather a tremendous amount of data and must interpret it quickly. As a result, autonomous vehicles need deep learning systems, high-performance processing, and sophisticated algorithms to adapt to changing conditions. This implies that the software, not the actual vehicle or truck, is the key. Cars with advanced software can adapt their guidance systems to changing roads, weather, and driving circumstances by learning from other vehicles' experiences on the road.

Criminal law and justice

The field of criminal justice is utilizing AI. The city of Chicago has created a "Strategic Subject List" powered by AI that assesses individuals who have been arrested for their likelihood of committing crimes again. On a scale of 0 to 500, it ranks 400,000 individuals based on factors like age, criminal history, victimization, drug-related arrest histories, and gang membership. Analyzing the data, analysts discovered that drug arrests are not significantly linked to future criminal behavior, being a victim of a gunshot is connected with being a future perpetrator, and youth is a powerful predictor of violence.

According to judicial experts, AI programs make punishment more equitable and less biased against people in law enforcement. Caleb Watney, associate at R Street Institute, writes:

Predictive risk analysis problems with an empirical foundation highlight the benefits of AI technologies such as automated reasoning and machine learning. According to a machine-learning policy simulation, these kinds of systems might be used to lower crime rates by up to 24.8 percent while maintaining the same jail population, or lower jail populations by up to 42 percent while maintaining the same crime rates.

Critics are concerned, meanwhile, that AI algorithms could be "a secret system to punish citizens for crimes they haven't committed." Large-scale roundups have been guided by the risk scores on multiple occasions. The worry is that these instruments unfairly single out individuals of color and haven't done anything to stop the murderous spree that has hit Chicago in recent years.

Despite these reservations, some nations are proceeding with swift deployment in this field. To assist them in improving their technology, Chinese corporations, for instance, already have "considerable resources and access to voices, faces, and other biometric data in vast quantities." Artificial Intelligence (AI) can be applied to these integrated data sets to enhance national security and law enforcement by matching sounds and photos with other kinds of information. This is made possible by new technologies.

Chinese law enforcement is creating a "police cloud" by combining video footage, travel records, social media activity, internet transactions, and personal identities through its "Sharp Eyes" program. Authorities can monitor lawbreakers, potential lawbreakers, and terrorists thanks to this integrated database.27 Stated differently, China has emerged as the world's top surveillance state that utilizes AI.

Health care

Healthcare designers are benefiting from AI tools that increase computational sophistication. For instance, the German business Merantix uses deep learning to address medical problems. "Detects lymph nodes in the human body in Computer Tomography (CT) images" is one of its uses in medical imaging. Its researchers say that marking the nodes and spotting little growths or lesions that might be troublesome is crucial. Although radiologists charge $100 per hour and may only be able to carefully read four photos in an hour, humans are capable of doing this. This method would cost $250,000 if there were 10,000 photos, which is unaffordable if done by humans.

In this case, deep learning can be used to teach computers through data sets what distinguishes a normal-looking lymph node from one that appears irregularly. Radiological imaging specialists can then use this knowledge to assess a patient's risk of malignant lymph nodes by applying it to real patients through imaging exercises and improving labeling accuracy. The trick is to distinguish between the unhealthy and healthy nodes because only a small percentage of them are likely to test positive.

AI has also been used to treat congestive heart failure, a condition that affects 10% of the elderly and costs the US economy $35 billion annually. The reason AI technologies are beneficial is that they "allocate resources to patient education, sensing, and proactive interventions that keep patients out of the hospital and predict in advance potential challenges ahead.

Conclusion

The majority of individuals do not have much familiarity with artificial intelligence (AI). For example, in a 2017 survey of 1,500 senior corporate executives in the US, only 17% claimed to be familiar with artificial intelligence.1. Many of them had no idea what it was or how it would impact their specific businesses. They were aware that AI had a great deal of potential to change business procedures, but they were unsure about how to implement AI in their own companies.

Artificial Intelligence (AI) is a technology that is revolutionizing all aspects of life, even though it is not well known. With the help of this versatile tool, people can reconsider how we combine data, evaluate it, and apply the new understanding to make better decisions. With this thorough review, we seek to enlighten policymakers, thought leaders, and interested parties about artificial intelligence (AI) and show them how it is already changing the world and posing significant issues for governance, the economy, and society.